Nurse Gifts For Women

Made in the USA
Columbia, SC
14 June 2020

10829812R00059